BONES

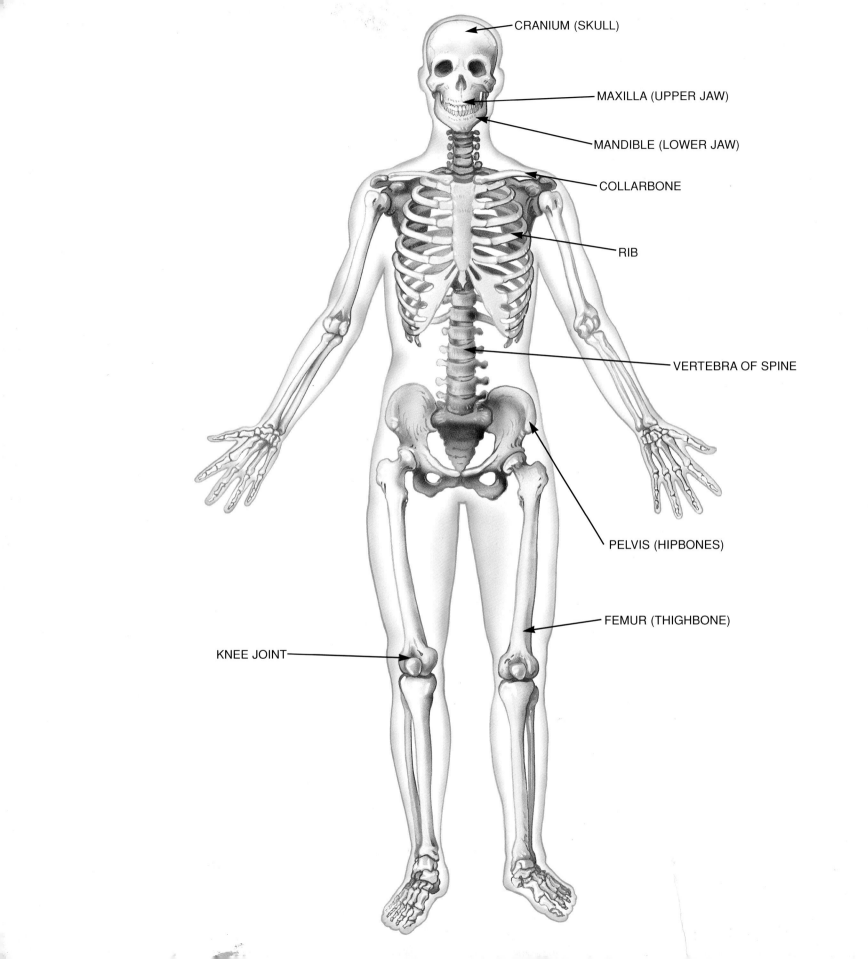

CRANIUM (SKULL)

MAXILLA (UPPER JAW)

MANDIBLE (LOWER JAW)

COLLARBONE

RIB

VERTEBRA OF SPINE

PELVIS (HIPBONES)

FEMUR (THIGHBONE)

KNEE JOINT

BONES

Our Skeletal System

Seymour Simon

MORROW JUNIOR BOOKS
New York

Photography Note

Scientists are using fantastic new machines that peer inside the human body to picture the invisible and help doctors save lives. In this book, we see extraordinary views of the interior of the human body. Many of these images were taken by various kinds of scanners, which change X-ray photos into computer code to make clear, colorful graphics. The computer-enhanced pictures of planets beamed back to Earth from distant space use a similar technique. These new ways of seeing help all of us to understand and appreciate that most wonderful machine: the human body.

The author would like to thank Orli R. Etingin, M.D., for her careful reading of the manuscript of this book.

PHOTO AND ART CREDITS
Permission to use the following photographs is gratefully acknowledged: front jacket, Howard Sochurek; page 6, Martin Dohrn/Science Photo Library; back jacket and pages 9, 32, P. Motta/Department of Anatomy, University La Sapienza, Rome/Science Photo Library; pages 10-11, Andrew Syred/Science Photo Library; pages 13, 18, VU/SIU; page 17, John Watney/Photo Researchers, Inc.; page 20, John Bavosi/Science Photo Library; pages 22, 28, Science Photo Library; page 25, L. Bassett/Video Surgery; page 26, CRNI/Science Photo Library; page 31, Chris Bjornberg/Photo Researchers, Inc.
Art on pages 2 and 15 by Ann Neumann.

The text type is 18-point Garamond Book.

Published by Morrow Junior Books
a division of William Morrow and Company, Inc.
1350 Avenue of the Americas, New York, NY 10019
www.williammorrow.com

Printed in Singapore at Tien Wah Press.

1 2 3 4 5 6 7 8 9 10

Library of Congress Cataloging-in-Publication Data
Simon, Seymour.
Bones: our skeletal system/Seymour Simon.
p. cm.
Summary: Describes the skeletal system and outlines the many important roles that bones play in the healthy functioning of the human body.
ISBN 0-688-14644-9 (trade)—ISBN 0-688-14645-7 (library)
1. Bones—Juvenile literature. 2. Skeleton—Juvenile literature. [1. Bones. 2. Skeleton.]
I. Title. QP88.2.S52 1998 612.7'5—dc21 97-44751 CIP AC

To Joyce and her wonderful grandchildren:

Joel, Benjamin, and Chloe

Your bones are like the framework of a building. Without a framework, the building would collapse. Without a skeleton, your body would be nothing more than a heap of muscles and soft tissue. If you didn't have bones, you wouldn't be able to stand, walk, or run.

Bones not only support your body, they also protect important organs in your body. The bones of your skull protect your brain, while those in your spine protect the nerves in your spinal cord. Your ribs protect your heart, lungs, and stomach.

Bones may seem lifeless, but they are actually made of cells and are living parts of your body. Bones grow and change just as you do. You begin life with about three hundred bones in your body. As you get older, some of those bones join together, so that by the time you are an adult you will have only about two hundred six bones.

Bones are mostly made up of flat plates called lamellae.

Bones are strong yet light. Before we are born, our bones are solid. Gradually some become hollow, which makes them very light, but hollow bones are still strong.

As our bodies develop in the womb, our bones are made of a soft, flexible material called cartilage. By the time we are born, much of this cartilage has hardened and turned to bone. New bone tissue is constantly being made. Minerals that we get from food make the bones as hard as rock. Strong, stringy material called collagen also runs through most bones and toughens them.

The bones are a storage place for minerals. If certain minerals are needed by other parts of the body, they are released from the bones into the blood. Up until the age of thirty-five, there is more new bone being created than there is old bone breaking down. But by the time we reach old age, a lot of minerals and collagen have disappeared from our bones, which weakens them. These weak bones break more easily, so that elderly people often suffer from broken bones.

Many bones are hollow, making them very light yet still strong.

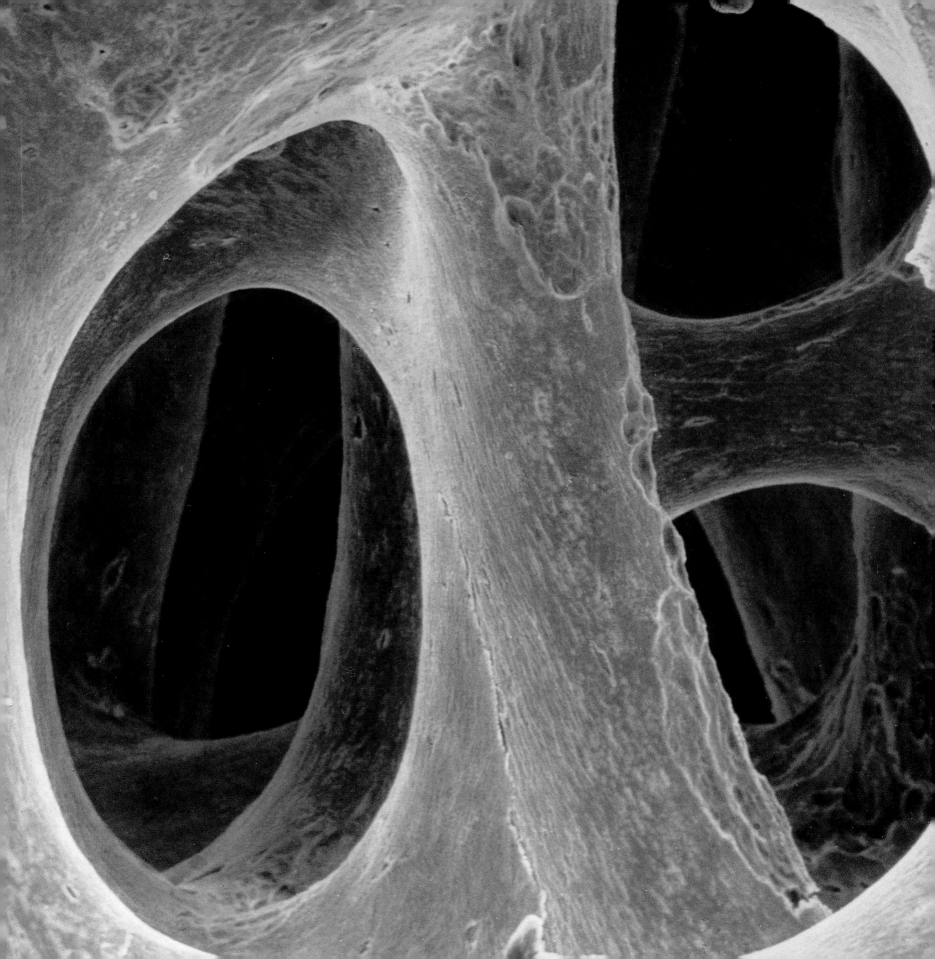

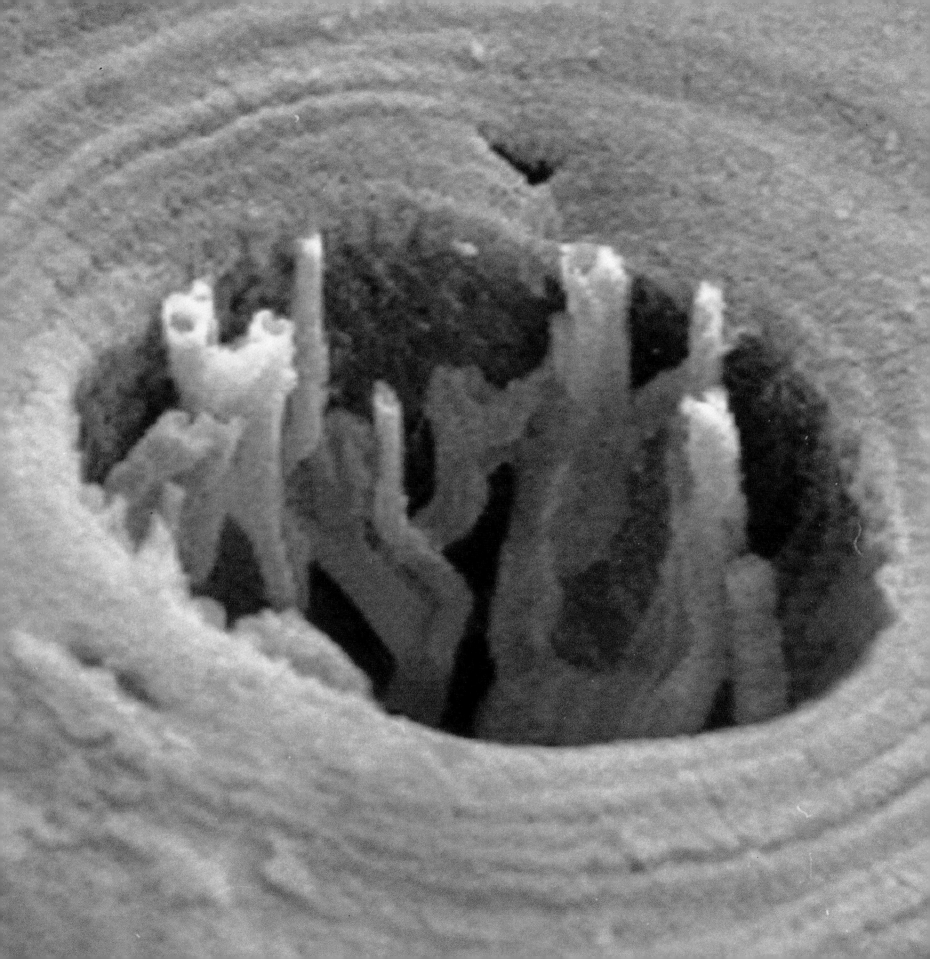

bone's outer layer is dense and tough and is called hard bone. It is made of living bone cells that form rings around tiny canals through which blood vessels pass. Inside the bone is a honeycomb of bone cells with spaces between them. This is called spongy bone.

The hollow centers of many bones are filled with jellylike red and yellow marrow. Yellow bone marrow stores fat and releases it when it is needed elsewhere in the body. Red bone marrow is a tissue that makes red and white blood cells and platelets in huge amounts—up to five thousand million red blood cells and thousands upon thousands of white blood cells and platelets each day. These cells all do vital jobs—the red blood cells carry oxygen throughout your body, the white blood cells fight disease and infection, and the platelets help the blood to clot after an injury.

In addition to storing minerals and forming blood cells, your bones are also working with your muscles and joints so that you can chew food, walk and run, twist and turn, or throw a ball. Wherever two bones come close to each other, there is a joint. In some places, such as the joints between the bones of the skull, the bones are locked together. But most joints are movable and are coated with a thick, slippery fluid much like the oil on a door hinge.

There are many types of movable joints, each of which moves differently. Ball-and-socket joints in the hip and shoulder allow free movement in all directions. Hinge joints in the elbows, knees, and fingers allow back-and-forth movement, like the hinges on a door.

Other types of joints, such as saddle, pivot, and sliding joints, allow many different movements. If a joint is twisted too much, it is said to be sprained or dislocated.

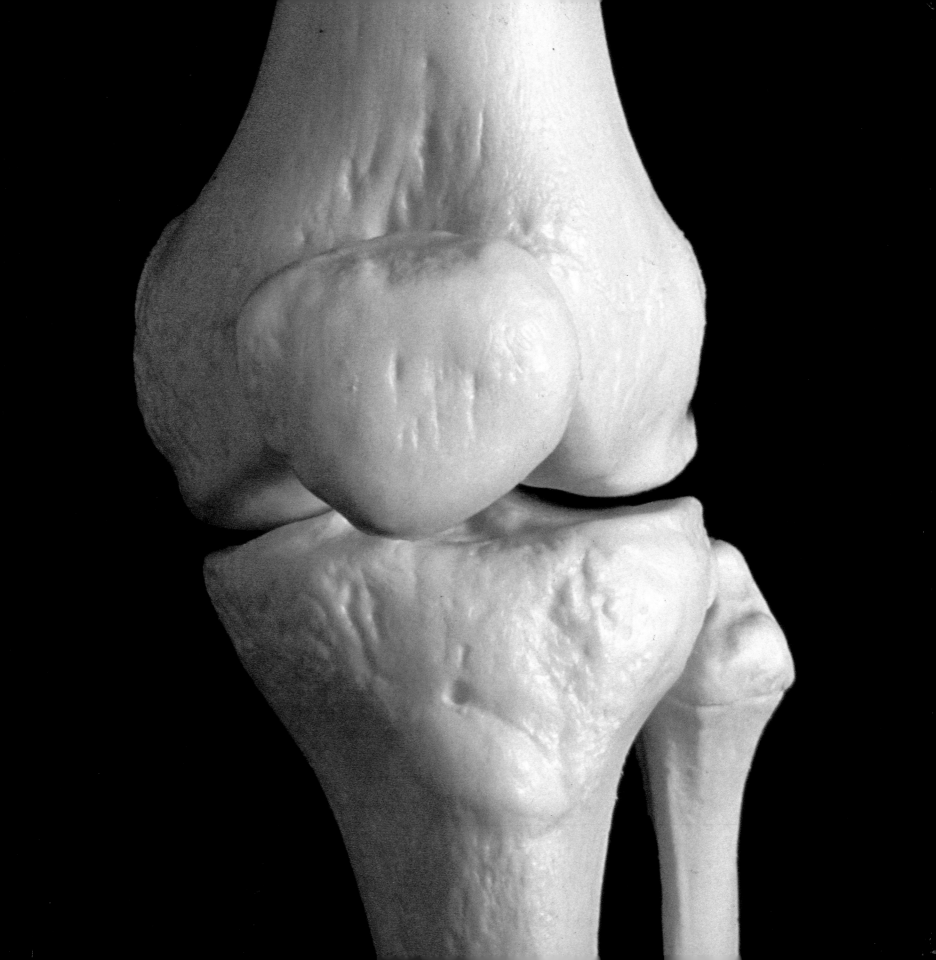

Bones are moved by muscles that are attached to them. The muscles are fastened to bones by tendons, which also link muscles to other muscles. For example, when you flex your arm, muscles pull together. The attached tendons pull against the bones of your arm, making them move at the joint. Tendon tissues stretch much less than muscles do. Most tendons are shaped like narrow cables.

Ligaments are like tendons but can stretch slightly. Ligaments link bones together at joints and are very strong. In some parts of the body, ligaments hold the bones together so tightly that they can barely move. Without ligaments, bones at joints would become dislocated very easily. A sprained ligament can be quite painful.

Cartilage is another kind of connective tissue found in joints and at the ends of bones. It's smooth, tough, and flexible and lets one bone slide over another. There are several different kinds of cartilage. Touch the tip of your nose or the top of your ear and you can feel one kind. Touch the voice box in your throat to feel another kind.

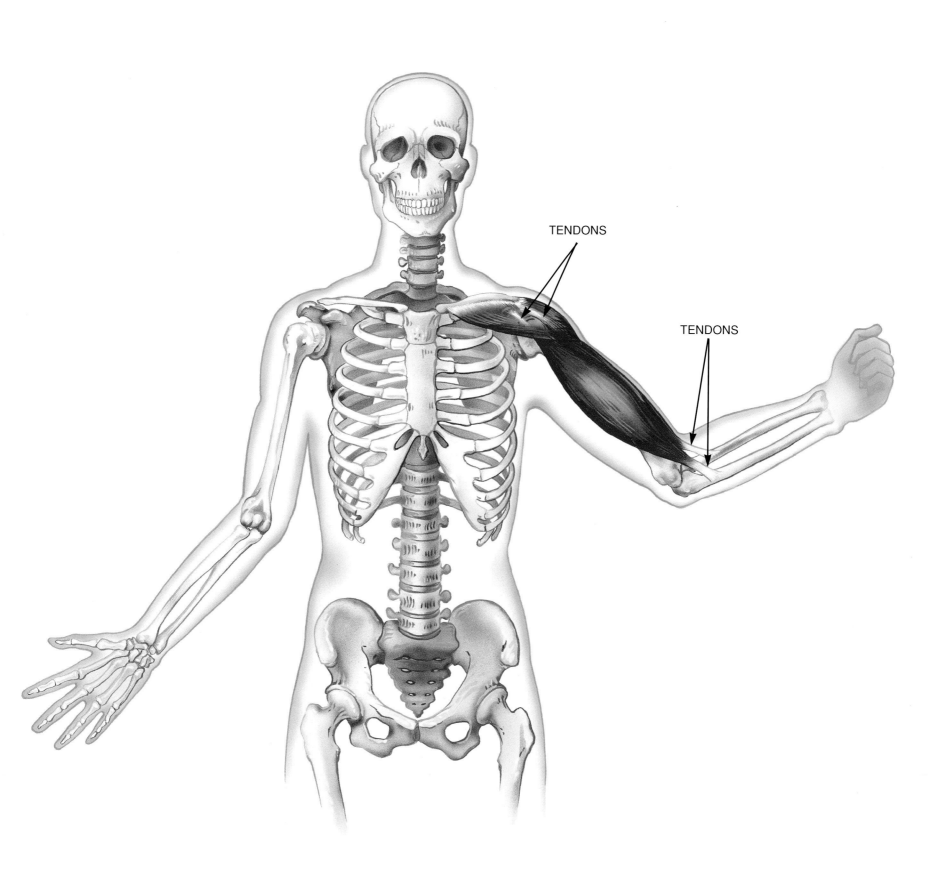

TENDONS

TENDONS

The skeleton is a column of interlinked bones, with two legs attached at the bottom and two arms and a skull attached at the top. The skull is a bony case that supports and protects the brain and some of the body's sense organs, such as the eyes and the ears. There are twenty-nine different bones in the skull, including small bones in each of the inner ears. The part of the skull that surrounds the brain is called the cranium. It is made up of eight interlocking cranial bones that enclose the brain and keep it from harm.

Fourteen facial bones form the framework for the eyes, nose, cheekbones, and upper and lower jaw. Looking at the skull, you can see how the deep eye sockets protect the delicate eyes. The part of the body that detects odors is also tucked away behind the nose hole, deep inside the skull.

Two bones form the upper jaw, or maxilla. These bones are attached to the rest of the skull and can't move. The lower jaw, or mandible, is hinged so that it can move up and down or side to side. The upper and lower jaws form a crusher that can bite, rip, and grind food into small pieces.

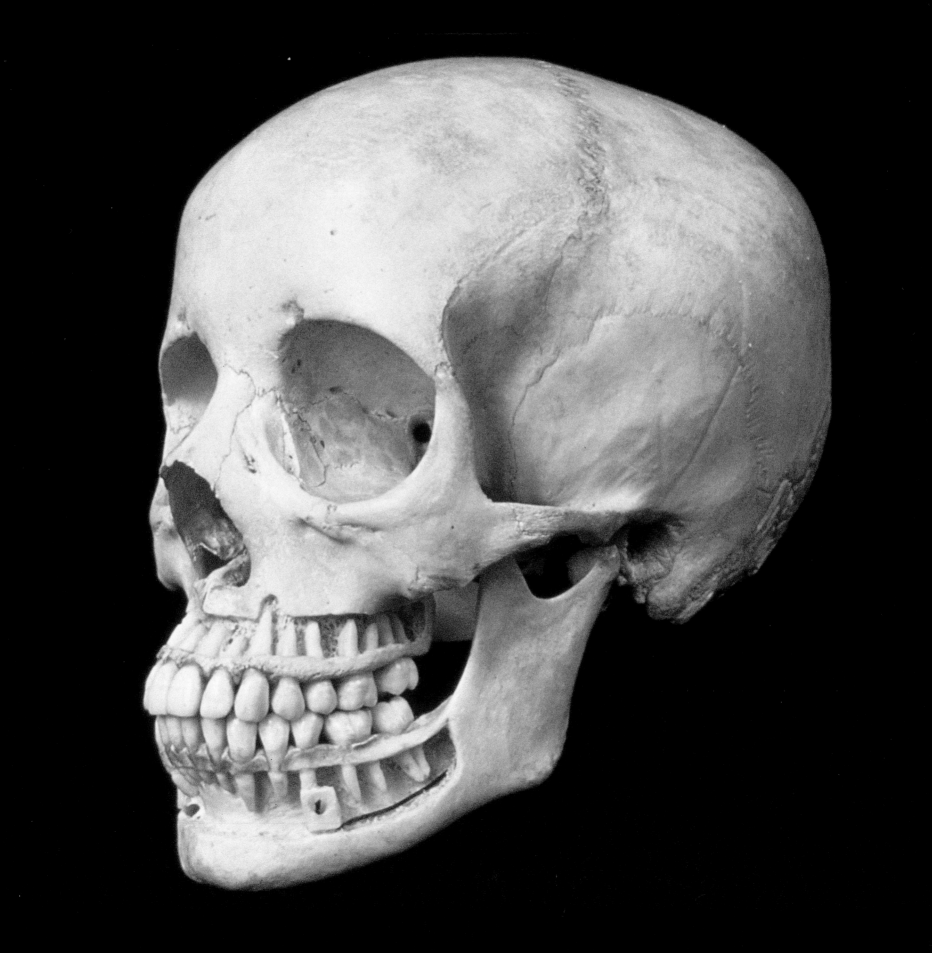

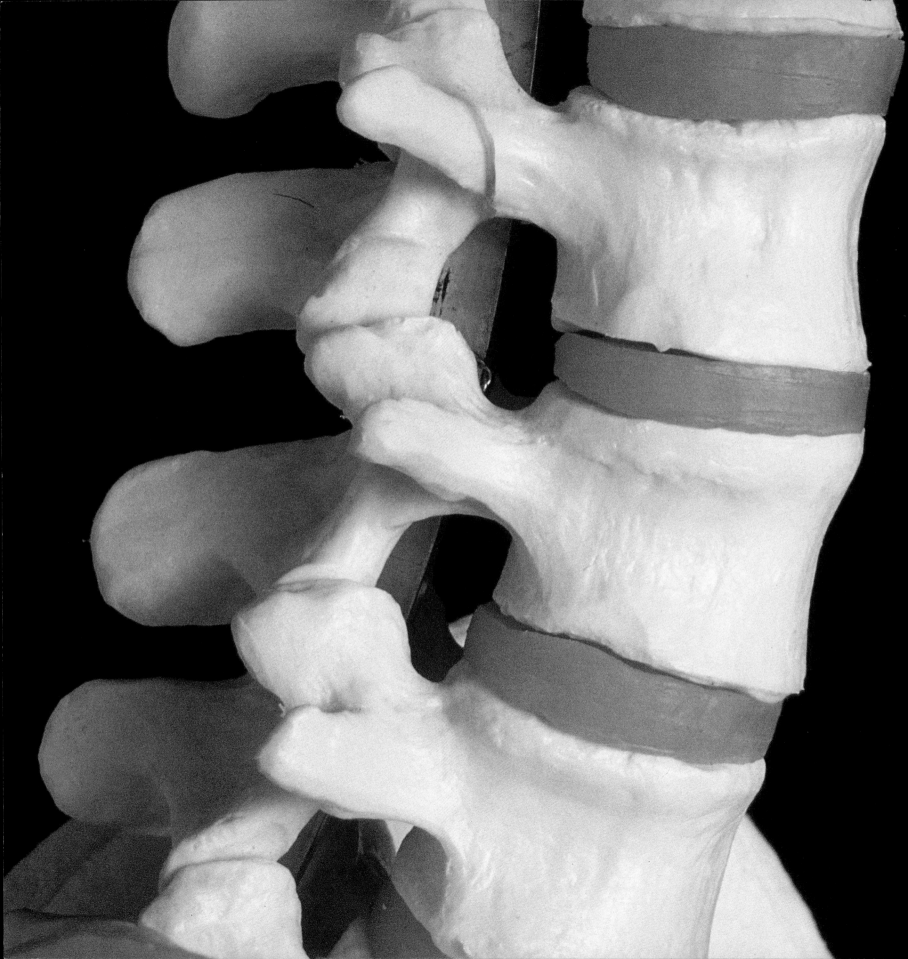

Your backbone, or spine, is a flexible column of bones that runs down the middle of your body. It is made up of a chain of thirty-three small bones called vertebrae, which are fastened one on top of another. Each vertebra is hard and hollow, like a bead or a spool of thread. The joint between each vertebra allows only a small amount of movement, but together the vertebrae form a flexible chain of bones that can twist like a string of beads. Your spine lets you bend down and touch your toes, and at the same time it keeps your body upright.

The vertebrae are cushioned by disks, which are like small circles of jelly between the bones. The spinal cord—a central bundle of nerves—runs through the hollow in the vertebrae. Individual nerves come out from the spinal cord and go through openings in the vertebrae to all parts of the body. A spinal disk that slips out of place or is injured can push through the surrounding cartilage, press on a spinal nerve, and cause great pain.

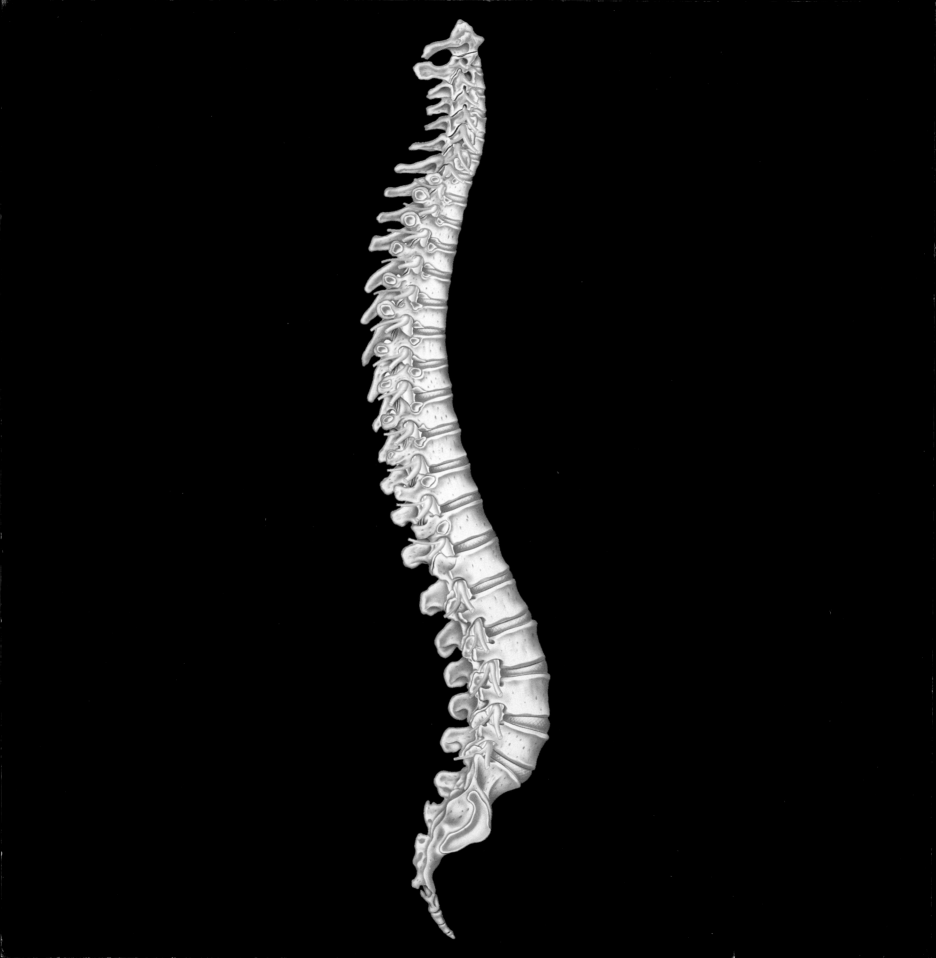

Seen from the side, your spine looks like an *S*, with four main curves. Two of the curves bend toward the back of your body and two bend toward the front. The curves help to strengthen your backbone, balance your body, and absorb shocks as you move.

Sometimes the curve of the spine is not what it should be because of the position of the bones or of the spinal muscles. Scoliosis is an abnormal curvature of the spine sometimes found in children. A mild case of scoliosis can be so slight that it is not even noticed by the person who has it. However, severe cases can produce pain and difficulty of movement.

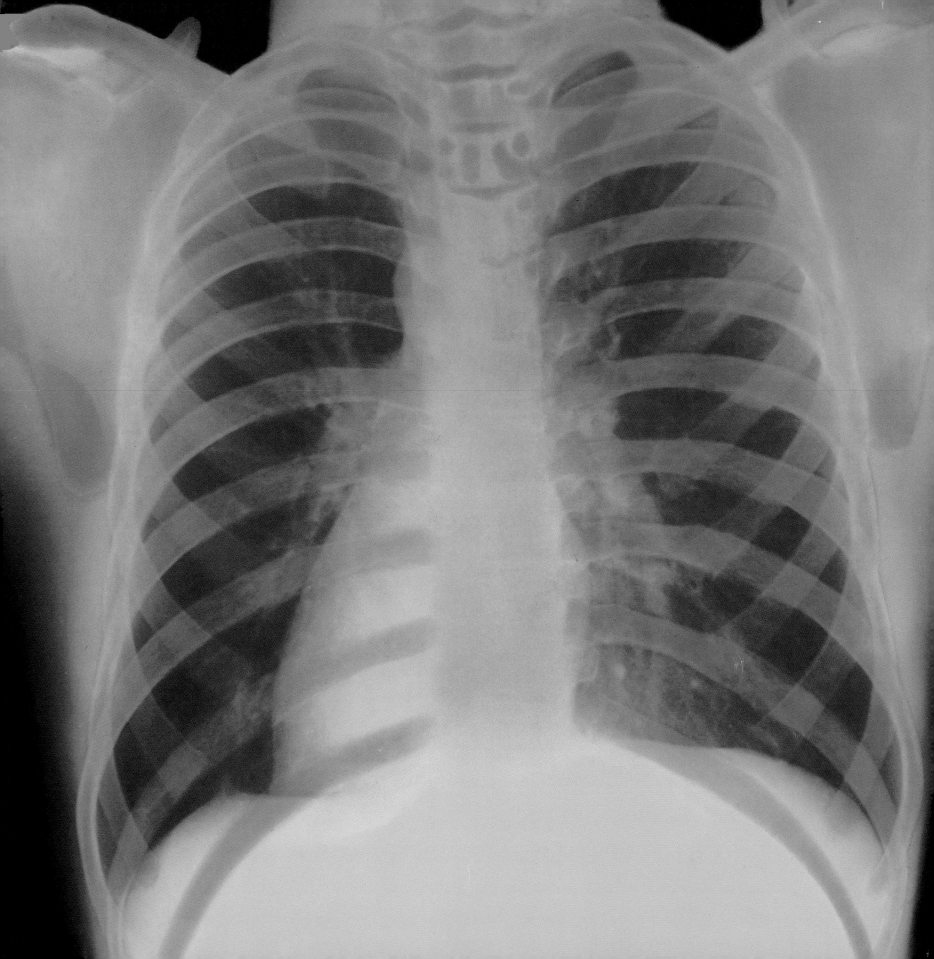

Your rib cage forms a protective shell for some of your most important organs, including your heart, lungs, stomach, and liver. The cage is made up of twelve pairs of curved bones called ribs. The top seven pairs of ribs are connected to the breastbone, at the front of the chest, by strips of cartilage. The next three pairs, called false ribs, are connected to the ribs above. The rear end of each rib is attached to a vertebra. The lower two pairs, called floating ribs, are not attached to the ribs above them but only to the backbone.

Breathe in as deeply as you can, and notice how your chest expands and relaxes. It rises up and outward as you inhale air into your lungs, then down and inward when you exhale. Your chest muscles underneath your ribs move your rib cage each time you breathe.

During hard physical exercise, the chest muscles force the chest to expand further by pushing the breastbone outward. This brings more air, which we need to keep exercising, into the lungs and to the muscles.

There are many different kinds of bones in your arms, legs, hands, and feet. Some are bound together by cartilage and can barely move, while others can move easily.

The femur, or thighbone, in the leg is the longest and heaviest bone in the body. The leg is attached to the spine by the pelvis, a group of strong bones. The bottom of the thighbone forms the upper part of the knee. The two bones in the lower part of each leg are attached to the knee at the top and the foot at the bottom. The foot is made up of an arrangement of small bones that flexes when we walk.

The knee joint, which connects the thighbone to the lower leg bones, is the biggest and strongest single joint in the body. It has the ability to lock the leg in a straight line and bear the weight of your entire body when you stand. It also bends, so that you can walk. Try walking without bending your knees to see how stiff-legged and unnatural it feels. A knee injury is one of the most serious injuries that a sports player can suffer, because it affects the speed and agility of the player.

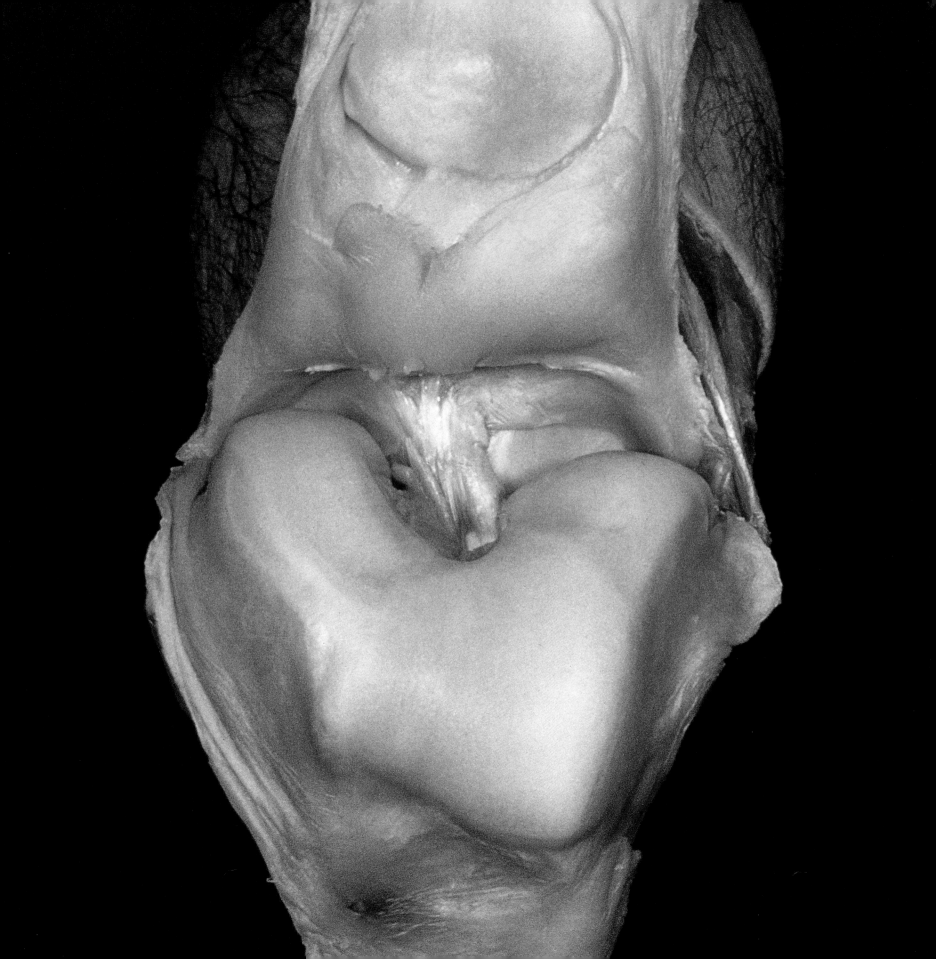

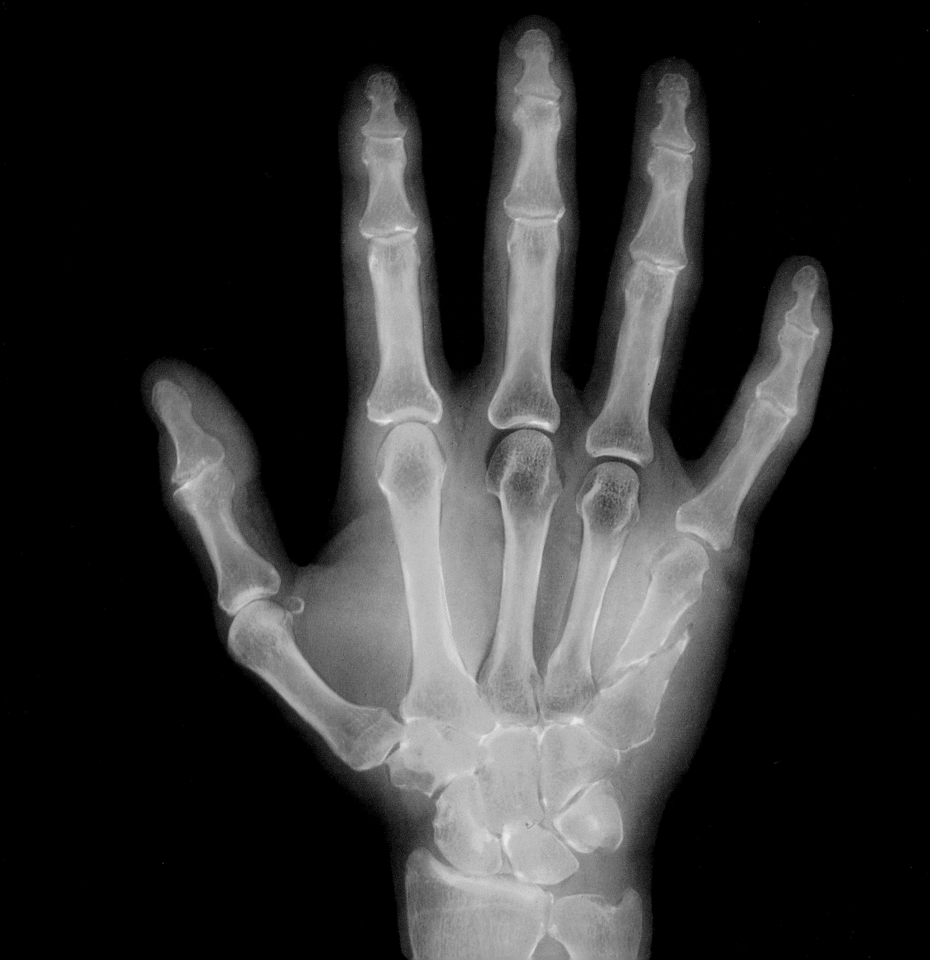

The bones of the arm are connected at the top to the collarbone and the shoulder bone, and at the bottom to the hands. Your hands are very powerful and very flexible. They are strong enough to carry a heavy book, yet delicate enough to turn one page at a time.

The hand has twenty-seven bones in three groups: the phalanges in the fingers and thumbs, the carpals in the wrist, and the metacarpals in the palm. There are fourteen finger bones—three in each finger and two in the thumb. The joints in the fingers are called knuckles. The wrist is made up of eight small bones arranged in two rows and held tightly together with ligaments. Five long bones make up the palm. Each of these bones is connected by joints to a finger bone at one end and to a wrist bone at the other.

All of these bones and joints allow us to bend our hands in almost any direction and at any angle.

This X-ray photo of a hand reveals a broken bone. Can you find the break?

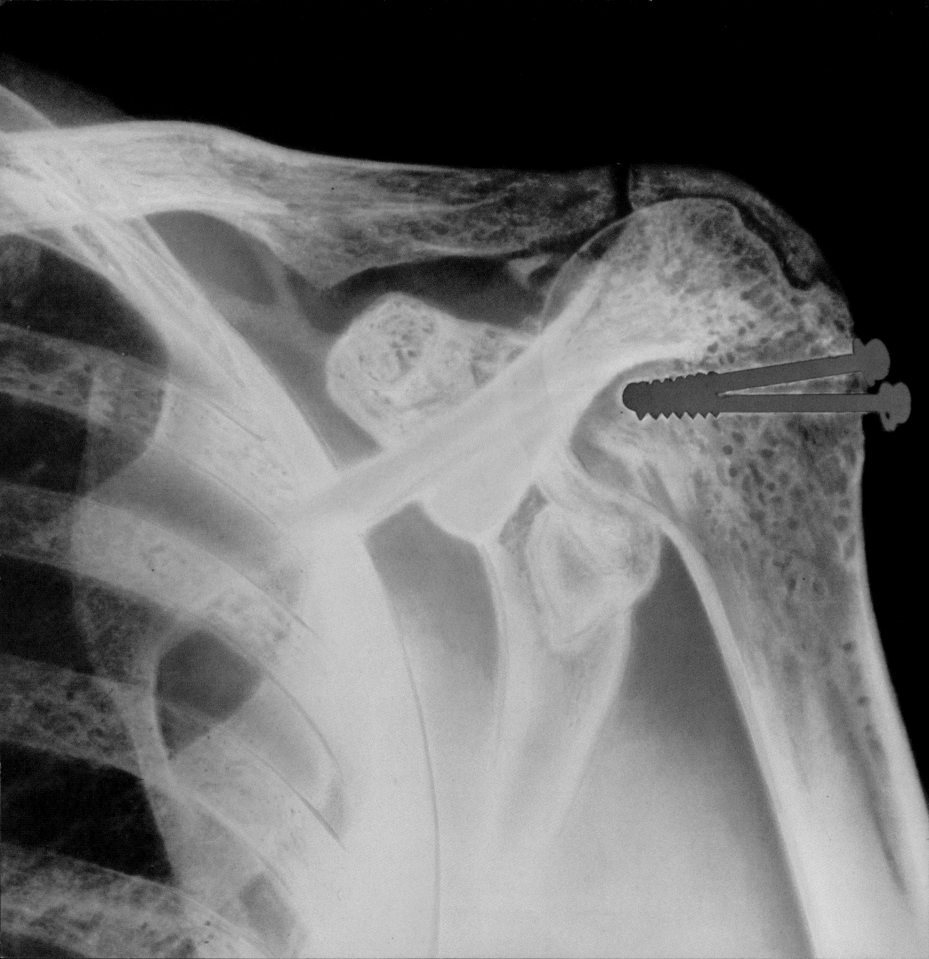

At times bad things happen to bones. A bone put under a lot of pressure may break, or fracture. There are two main kinds of fractures: a compound fracture, in which the bone is shattered or pushes through the skin, and a simple fracture, in which the broken bone does not pierce the skin.

Amazingly enough, broken bones can often repair themselves. All bones are covered by a thin protective layer called a periosteum, except at the joints. This layer contains tiny blood vessels and cells that repair damaged bones.

If a bone is broken, a blood clot forms to seal the space between the broken ends. About two days later, bone cells from the periosteum move in and begin to close up and seal the break with new bone.

Sometimes, though, broken bones need to be held together in order to heal properly. If the broken ends are lined up, the new bone will be as straight and long as it was before it was broken. This colored X ray shows two metal screws that have been placed into a fractured upper arm bone to keep it from moving while it heals.

If a joint becomes injured and painful, doctors may try to repair it with a procedure called arthroscopy, which uses a long, thin instrument to view and repair a joint. They may also replace the joint entirely with an artificial one. A hip can be replaced with a metal ball that turns in a plastic socket. In knee replacements, a plastic-covered hinge is used to replace cartilage.

Arthritis is the name given to a number of diseases in which there is swelling of the joints. Osteoarthritis occurs mostly in older people, as cartilage wears down in the joints of the fingers, knees, and hips. These joints then become swollen, making movement difficult and painful. Middle-aged people often experience rheumatoid arthritis, which creates pain and stiffness in the joints. Rheumatism is the name given to any condition that produces pain or stiffness in joints and muscles. Doctors often treat simple rheumatism and arthritis with medicines that reduce swelling and pain. They usually perform joint replacement operations only in the most serious cases of arthritis.

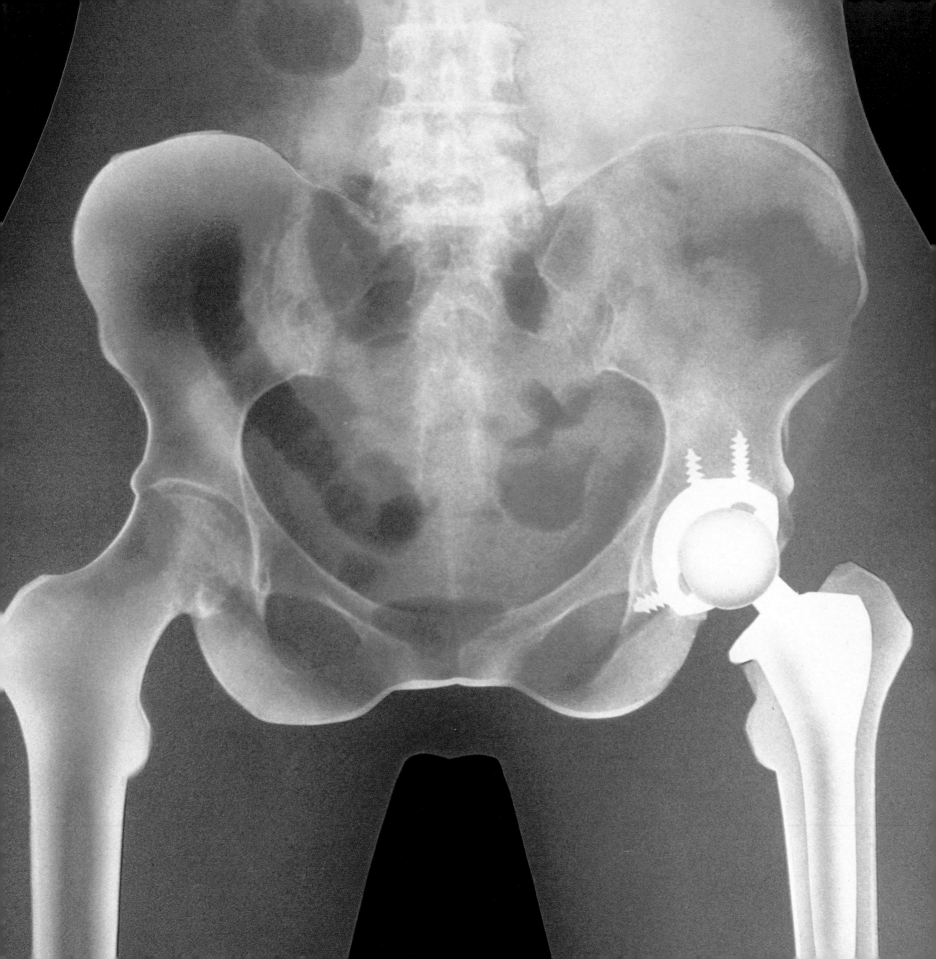

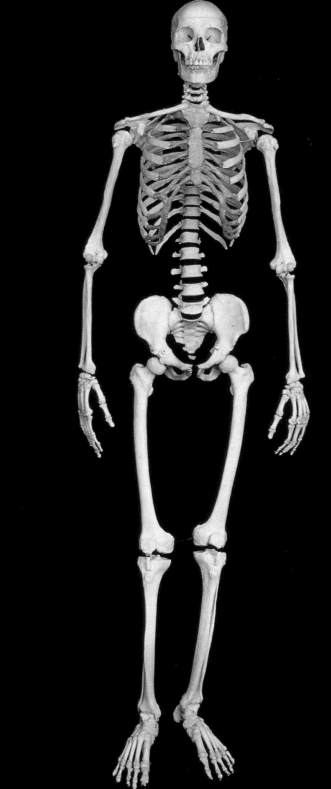

Bones are vital, living parts of your body. As old bone tissue breaks down in your body, new tissue is constantly forming. Your bones are as strong and tough as concrete and can bear heavy weights without bending or breaking. Your bones allow you to walk, run, eat, and breathe. They work with your muscles and the rest of your body to make you the marvelous living machine that you are.